Seasons

MW00608188

Contents

Spring 2

Summer. 4

Fall 6

Winter. 8

Seasons. 10

Index 12

Rigby

What can you see
in spring?

What can you see in summer?

What can you see in fall?

What can you see
in winter?

Spring

Summer

Fall

Winter

a b c d e f g h i j k l m n o p q r s t u v w x y z

Index

fall 6, 11

spring 2, 10

summer 4, 10

winter 8, 11